First published 2011
This edition © Wooden Books Ltd 2011

Published by Wooden Books Ltd.
8A Market Place, Glastonbury, Somerset

British Library Cataloguing in Publication Data
Creightmore, R.
Feng Shui

A CIP catalogue record for this book is
available from the British Library

ISBN 978 1904263 86 9

Printed and bound in Shanghai, China
by Shanghai iPrinting Co., Ltd.
100% recycled papers.

CONTENTS

INTRODUCTION

Feng Shui, literally "wind water", is the study of people's relationship with their living environment. Geomancy means "to divine the Earth'. Feng Shui encompasses the entire spectrum of Chinese geomantic practices and includes in its full scope the landscape design of dwellings, work-places, villages, cities, palaces, temples and graves. It is rooted in Daoist and Confucian philosophy and practicality.

The term *Kan Yu* predates the term Feng Shui; *Kan* represents Heaven and by extension higher areas, and *Yu* Earth and lower areas of land. It is a fundamental precept of ancient Chinese philosophy that humanity is in the position of being the intermediary between Heaven and Earth, and thrives when it learns to balance these two forces. A *Kan Yu* practitioner works ceremonially with the spirits of Earth and Heaven, and is expert in astrology, architecture, economics, geography, hydrology, landscape design, interior design, medicine, sociology, structural engineering and town planning. A related term is *Xiang Di*, the practical geographical appraisal of the landscape, involving hunting, agriculture, travel and warfare as well as building dwellings and towns. Most ancient sites in China were located on raised grounds near rivers, where fish and water could be obtained without danger of flooding. The common-sense practice of *Xiang Di* helped the ancients to select the best sites for settlement, and provided the basic principles of subsequent good Feng Shui practice.

This book presents a comprehensive and practical distillation of the essential elements of this venerable tradition. Feng Shui is at once an earth science, a magical tradition and an aesthetic art.

HISTORY
the development of geomantic ideas

During the Zhou Dynasty [1046-256 BC] a dwelling's fortune was often determined by *Zhen Pu*—divination by scapulimancy (using the shoulder blades of an ox). In the Warring States period [475-221 BC], use of the *Yi Jing* (*I Ching*) became popular, and Daoism, Confucianism, and the theories of *Yin* and *Yang*, *Wu Xing* (Five Elements) and *Ba Gua* (Eight Trigrams) began to take shape. By the time of the Han dynasty [206 BC-220 AD] written records of Feng Shui consultations appear. The first use of the term *Feng Shui* is attributed to Guo Pu of the Jin Dynasty [265-420 AD], who wrote in the *Zang Zhu* (*Book of Burial*):

> *"The dead should take advantage of the Sheng Qi. The wind will disperse the Qi and the water will contain it. The ancients said that one should try to gather the Qi so that it will not disperse. The aim is to keep it flowing but contained. Hence it is called Feng Shui."*

Feng Shui thus means the art of understanding movement and stillness in the land:

> *"Without water Qi disperses when there is wind, with water Qi stills and wind disappears... It follows that the best sites are those with water, then follow sites that are sheltered from the wind." (Fan Yu Bing)*

Since the Song Dynasty [960-1279 AD], two main schools of Feng Shui have evolved: the *Xing Shi Pai* or *Forms School*, based on the subjective observation of the physical world, and the *Li Qi Pai* or *Compass School*, based on the objective observation of the subtle and intangible world using the *Luopan* or Feng Shui Compass. Both are used together in practice to determine the auspiciousness of a site.

Above: Emperor Da Yu, a Kan Yu expert and water diviner, with dowsing instrument. Left: Traditional divination using a tortoise carapace and yarrow stalks.

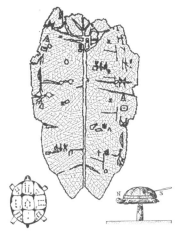

Above: Calculating the equinox using a gnomon. Left: Early style of divination by heating a tortoiseshell or ox scapula in the fire and reading the cracks.

THREE GIFTS AND FIVE LUCKS
between heaven and earth

The fundamental triad of Daoist metaphysical philosophy is of the *Three Gifts* (*San Cai*)—Heaven (*Tian*), Earth (*Di*) and Humankind (*Ren*). These encompass all aspects of Feng Shui, and are often found symbolised in tripartite architectural plans and forms. The Temple of Heaven in Beijing has three principal buildings each with an altar to one of the Three Gifts (*e.g. the Imperial Vault of Heaven, opposite top*).

Also central to Daoist philosophy are the *Five Lucks*. In order of importance these represent five variables in the human experience of life. *Destiny* (*Ming*), includes the concepts of destiny inherited from ancestry and also the Ming of a site—every site has its timely rightful owner. *Luck* (*Yun*, timing) distinguishes between the luck every human creates and the luck over which one has no control. *Feng Shui* is centrally concerned with the external environment and how it can reflect the internal environment (and vice versa), and thus is one of the Eight Limbs of traditional Chinese Medicine (it is a basic tenet that an alteration to the external form of a home will cause an internal shift within its inhabitants, so a Feng Shui cure can affect the other four Lucks, including Destiny). *Virtue* (*Yin De*) represents good deeds and service to others. Finally, *Knowledge* (*Du Shu*) represents education and self-cultivation.

Daoist philosophy perceives a unity in which every being, living and dead, is connected, and most strongly within a family lineage, so the destinies of descendants are influenced by ancestors' graves (*e.g. Ming Imperial tombs centre opposite*) and the destinies of ancestors by the provision of good house sites for their descendants.

		Astronomy
		Astrology
	Cosmic Qi	Moon & Stars
		The "Yi Jing"
Heavenly Qi		Time & Cycles
		Rain
		Sunlight
	Weather Qi	Heat & Cold
		Wind
		Seasons
		Tides
		Mountains
		Valleys & Plains
	Topographical Qi	Rivers and Streams
		Magnetic Fields
		Di Mai (Earth
Earthly Qi		Meridians)
		Orientations
		Dwellings
	Environmental Qi	Manmade Objects
		Form and Space
		Colour & Sound
		Furniture Layout
		Political
		Cultural
	Social Qi	Social Contacts
		Neighbours
		Family + Relatives
Human Qi		Partner
		Memories
		Ideals & Visions
	Personal Qi	Personality
		Sensitivity
		Vital Qi

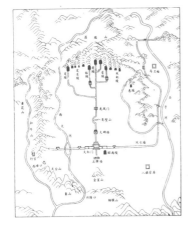

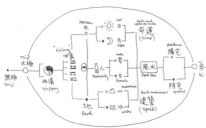

"The Dao gave birth to One, One gave birth to Two, Two gave birth to Three, Three gave birth to the ten thousand things." Dao De Jing Ch.2.
Dao, or "the way", is understood as a pantheistic composite of, and the intrinsic order within all things.

5

QI
breaths of life

The life-breath of Dao is *Qi* ("chi"), often translated as 'energy' though more precisely 'breaths of life'. *Qi* is understood as permeating Heaven and Earth, all things living and transforming because of *Qi*. *Sheng Qi* (creative, fertile Qi) is the harmonious expression of *Yin* and *Yang*, the physical phenomenon of vitality; it is *Qi* in motion constantly in all things. In contrast, *Sha Qi* is harmful environmental *Qi* which can range from noxious earth radiations and other physical phenomena (*see pages 38-41*) to subtle psychological and astrological threats. The aim of Feng Shui is to seek the time, space and direction of healthy *Sheng Qi* and avoid or transform unhealthy *Sha Qi*.

> *'Feng Shui values Qi of the mountains and rivers as they are the backbones of the Earth. Mountains congeal because of Qi, Qi becomes obvious because of mountains'* - Di Li Wu Jue, Zhao Jiu Feng.

The geographical aspect of life energy is termed *Di Qi* or Earth Energy, and places that are congenial for plant growth and human habitation have good *Di Qi*. Biological health is subtly influenced by rock and soil quality, dampness, the Earth's magnetic fields, and radiations from minerals, geological faults and underground streams.

Qi Yun (*Qi Timing*) is the state and passage of *Qi* in time and space, derived from *Xiang Di* (appraisal of land) and Astrology (consideration of timing): Earth rotates and Heavenly *Qi* (weather) follows it; Heaven moves and Earth *Qi* is affected. A piece of land with good Feng Shui will not always remain so: timely use of the site is important. Similarly not everyone can benefit from a good site as each has its rightful owner, according to their personal astrology.

Left: A Dragon-shaped mountain, a very beneficial simulacrum. Centre: Accumulated Qi, the ideal configuration of topographical features, mountains and rivers around the Long Xue, or Dragon's Lair, the most favourable site.   Right: "Hidden Qi is Qi that is intact.."

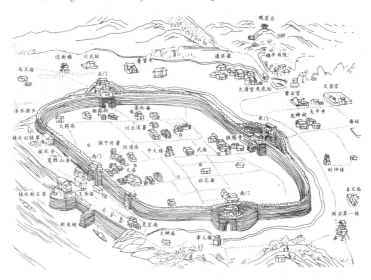

Above: The Qi Cang is an area where Qi converges and congregates, a discrete and precious space like a jewel box, within which Yin Qi and Yang Qi can interact and harmonise.

7

Shan Shui

mountains and water

Qi circulates throughout the earth in varying ways depending on local geodesic forces and topography. The *Long Mai* or *Dragon Meridian* is a current of concentrated Earth *Qi* that emanates the valuable *Long Qi* or *Dragon's Breath*. Long undulating mountain chains are thus seen as major *Mountain Dragons*, and large rivers as major *Water Dragons*. Majestic mountains embody *Yang Qi* (the higher the land the stronger its *Qi*), while meandering water is *Yin Qi* (the deeper the water, the bigger its *Qi*). Dragons link all features in the landscape, and are considered the most important. Where the Dragon *Qi* is big, a capital city may develop; where it is small, only a town will thrive. The Dragon trunk becomes cities and towns, and its feet become villages.

Heavenly Qi descends from above into Mountain Dragons below, following the spines of their ranges, and flowing through their ridges, branches and formations like arteries. As it flows it either scatters and dissipates or is held and condensed by water *Qi*, for *Shan* (mountain) is like a host and *Shui* (water) its guest. When *Qi* circulates through landforms, landscape entities are thereby given life.

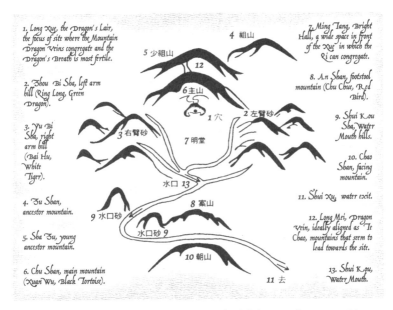

1. Long Xue, the Dragon's Lair, the focus of site where the Mountain Dragon Veins congregate and the Dragon's Breath is most fertile.

2. Zhou Bi Sha, left arm hill (Qing Long, Green Dragon).

3. Yu Bi Sha, right arm hill (Bai Hu, White Tiger).

4. Zu Shan, ancestor mountain.

5. Sha Zu, young ancestor mountain.

6. Chu Shan, main mountain (Xuan Wu, Black Tortoise).

7. Ming Tang, Bright Hall, a wide space in front of the Xue in which the Qi can congregate.

8. An Shan, footstool mountain (Chu Chue, Red Bird).

9. Shui Kou Sha, Water Mouth hills.

10. Chao Shan, facing mountain.

11. Shui Xu, water exit.

12. Long Mei, Dragon Vein, ideally aligned as Te Chao, mountains that seem to lead towards the site.

13. Shui Kou, Water Mouth.

Above: Nomenclature of features around a site. Below left: location of prosperous cities. Below right: Principal Mountain and Water Dragons of China. Opposite left: Scattered Dragon veins, the ranges have no systematic pattern. Opposite right: An inlet with mountains gradually sloping into the sea, gathering the Qi of both Mountain and Water Dragons.

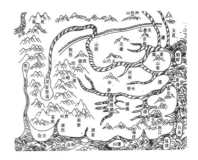

9

SHAN LONG
where Mountain Dragons roam

Mountain Dragon ranges are traditionally rated by the strength of their central *spine* and branches. Ideally, they "*should seem to be arriving from the distance in a never-ending manner*". Nestled beneath them, the best site for settlement is the *Long Xue,* or *Dragon's Lair*, located where the greatest number of beneficent Mountain Dragon veins congregate, and where the Dragon's breath is most fertile.

The end of the mountain range nearest any potential site is termed the *Head of the Dragon*, and the furthest end its *Tail*. The *Qi* can run forwards or backwards from the site according to the formation of the limbs. Gentle beginnings and endings of ranges are sought over abrupt ones as they allow space for the Dragon to develop, and for the *Qi* to gather where the *Mountain Long* merges into the plain. Cutting through a Mountain Dragon spine, e.g. for a road or rail cutting, can have a disastrous effect on the flow of *Qi,* and similarly damming a river can choke a Water Dragon. Footstool and facing mountains often usefully serve to balance excess *Yang* from high mountains to the rear, and to contain the *Ming Tang* (next page).

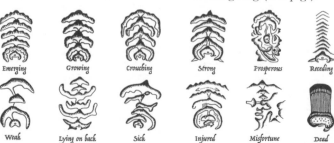

Emerging	Growing	Crouching	Strong	Prosperous	Receding
Weak	Lying on back	Sick	Injured	Misfortune	Dead

Convergence of Dragon's Breath at various Xue (marked as circles).

Barren, broken, rocky, excessive or solitary mountains destroy luck.

Mature Journeying Mountain Dragon nourishing the Xue (marked as circles).

Coherent Mountain Dragon veins surrounding the Xue.

SHUI LONG
there be Water Dragons

The *Ming Tang* is the open area in front of the *Xue*, ideally containing a river and fertile flood plain, in which the *Qi* can congregate and prosperity accumulate. The point where the water flows into the *Ming Tang* is known as the *Shui Kou* or *water mouth*, and the bigger the *Shui Kou* the greater the wealth it will encourage. Long, deep, slow, meandering watercourses are most conducive to the accumulation of Water Dragon *Qi*, particularly if they wind around seeming to embrace, and especially if they pool in front of the site. Water should be seen to linger as it flows away, with its exit point invisible from the site.

> *"With mountain one desires solidity. With water one desires clarity and stillness. The meandering of the emergent water compels high rank, abundance and wealth. If the mountain passes the water so that it winds, there will be a myriad of descendants. If the mountain causes the departure of water to be straight, one will be the servant of others or live with relatives because of straightened circumstances. If water passes from east to west, there will be endless wealth."* – Qing Wu, Burial Classic.

Sites on the outside of a bend or facing an oncoming current are at risk of inundation and therefore inauspicious, as are sites beside straight or fast-flowing streams which can conduct the *Qi* away from the site too rapidly. Joining streams are desirable as *Qi* concentrates. These Water Dragon precepts also apply to roads and paths.

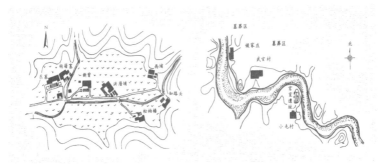

Above: Streams flowing east to west are favoured as they link the Dragon and Tiger, following the Sun. The best sites above are in the upper right of the left map and the centre of the right map. "The ideal site is nestled among watercourses protected in the belly of the Dragon" (Shui Long Jing).

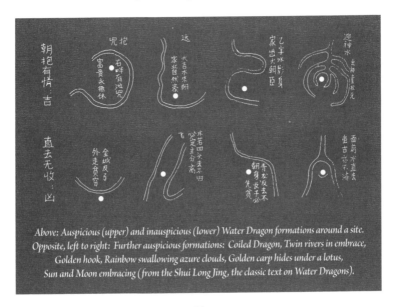

Above: Auspicious (upper) and inauspicious (lower) Water Dragon formations around a site.
Opposite, left to right: Further auspicious formations: Coiled Dragon, Twin rivers in embrace,
Golden hook, Rainbow swallowing azure clouds, Golden carp hides under a lotus,
Sun and Moon embracing (from the Shui Long Jing, the classic text on Water Dragons).

YIN YANG
defining each other

All Feng Shui is based on the balance of 陰 *Yin* and 陽 *Yang* in the environment. Even the ideograms are fundamentally rooted in the landscape, *Yang* meaning "the sunny side of the mountain" and *Yin* "the shady side". Healthy *Sheng Qi* (*see page 6*) accumulates best where *Yin* and *Yang* occur in a 40%-60% proportion.

Yin and *Yang* symbolise unity through the interaction of bipolar forces, essentially passive and active. Almost everything has a *Yin Yang* twin, for example night and day, Earth and Heaven, moon and sun, female and male, and birth and death. *Yin* and *Yang* qualities always exist in relation to each other, and are often further divided, elevation into high and low, and low into slightly raised (*Yang*) and flat (*Yin*). *Yin* and *Yang* also control and balance each other (if *Yang* is excessive then *Yin* will be weak and vice versa), and they create and transform into each other, this constant flux being the source of all change.

As *Yin* '—' and *Yang* '--' revolve they produce two sons and two daughters: the *Si Xiang* ("sir shang"), or *Four Celestial Spirits*:

⚎ *Shao (young) Yang* is east, spring, the green Dragon, the fixed stars, daylight, corporeality, rotation, unity in multiplicity, the Prince.

⚌ *Tai (old) Yang* is south, the red Phoenix, summer, heat, the sun, the eyes, duality or origin, the nature of things, the Monarch.

⚏ *Shao Yin* is west, autumn, the white Tiger, the planets, night, materiality, inertia, succession, multiplicity in unity, the Duke.

⚏ *Tai Yin* is north, winter, the dark Tortoise, the moon, the occult, passion, equality, the attributes of things, the Emperor ruling Earth.

Yin	Yang
EARTH	HEAVEN
MOON	SUN
DEPARTING	ARRIVING
STILLNESS	MOVEMENT
SLOW	FAST
NORTH	SOUTH
WEST	EAST
NIGHT	DAY
WET	DRY
DEAD	LIVE
WATER	FIRE
VALLEY	MOUNTAIN
INTERIOR	EXTERIOR
COLD	HOT
DECREASE	INCREASE
WINTER	SUMMER
AUTUMN	SPRING
EVEN	ODD
BLACK	WHITE
RECEPTIVE	CREATIVE
FEMALE	MALE

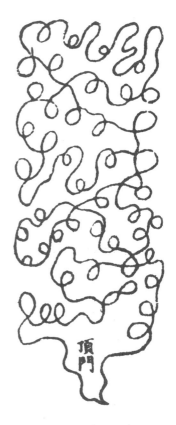

頂門

Above: Daoist meditation diagram:
The Blessed Union of Yin and Yang.

Top left: The Tai Ji, the Daoist Yin Yang
symbol, the circle representing the whole,
divided into Yin (black) and Yang (white),
each containing the seed of the other.

15

SI XIANG
the four Celestial Spirits

The *Four Spirits* simultaneously represent the four quarters of the ecliptic (or zodiac) and the topographic space around the *Xue*. To the north the black Tortoise (or dark turtle) represents the protective mountain wall behind the *Xue* whose strength is reflected in the prevailing health and social harmony of the residence where the earth *Qi* pools. To the south, the red Phoenix (or vermilion sparrow/pheasant) indicates the frontal area where the *Qi* is contained by the Phoenix (or water) wall, the open movement of *Qi* here reflecting in prosperity through the healthy flow of Heavenly and human *Qi* into the front door.

Traditionally this fundamental model is oriented with the Tortoise in the north, deriving from the practical benefits in China of facing sunshine from the south while being shielded from the cold winds of the north. Importantly however, this template can also be applied equally whatever the orientation of the landscape around a site. For example, in the case of a house with its back to a western mountain, the Tortoise is seen in the west, the Dragon in the north, the Tiger in the south, and the Phoenix and *Ming Tang* to the east.

The scheme may be similarly applied at other scales. In the urban landscape large surrounding buildings can substitute for mountain ranges. In domestic and commercial architecture the design may be represented in the shape of the built form within the plot. For example, in a bedroom the head of the bed should be against the most solid (Tortoise) wall of a room while facing the most active (Phoenix) wall, probably the one with the entrance or windows.

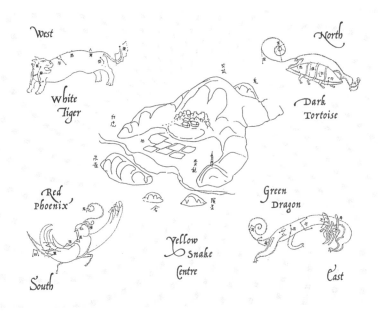

"In front there is a Red Bird followed by a slow moving Tortoise at the rear, to the left is the Azure Dragon and to the right a White Tiger" – the Li Ji (Book of Rites). *The centre is represented by a Yellow Snake.*

Above: Si Xiang principles visible in (from left to right): A traditional Chinese house, a fundamental Qi Gong posture, an armchair, and a Chinese grave. Central in all is the Ming Tang (or Bright Pool) in which the Qi can gather.

17

SI XIANG IN THE LANDSCAPE
animals all around

According to Feng Shui, the ideal formation around a site consists of a dark Tortoise, a strong high mountain range, behind but not too close, balanced by a red Phoenix, a lower range of hills or a single footstool hill in front. Meanwhile, to each side, the *Yang Qing* (azure or blue-green) Dragon and *Yin* white Tiger should meet in dynamic equilibrium. Specifically, the Dragon hill formation to the east should be craggy with a sense of movement, in contrast to the hills in the west which should be lower, rounder and more compact, much like a crouching Tiger.

Finding the Dragon is the key to finding the *Xue*. The Dragon is seen as dry and potent, its lines harsh and straight, its strength activating the earth, vitalising the soil and reanimating minerals for plants. The true green Dragon is a hill to the northeast, east or southeast, rising above the others with a sharp slope to its summit while on the other side it falls away more gently.

Where there is a true Dragon there is always a Tiger, for they are inseparable. The white Tiger current is moist and subtle, its lines soft, rounded and undulating. The realm of the Tiger lies in the foothills and lowlands, providing the fertile substance of the earth. A site's Dragon and Tiger will reflect in its male and female residents respectively, and the site is especially auspicious if the two embrace.

Above left: Dragon and Tiger flirting. Above right: Dragon and Tiger embracing
Below: Ideal Si Xiang formations, left to right, good, variant and best. Opposite left: Ideal
Tortoise, Phoenix, Dragon and Tiger formations cradling a site, improving left to right.

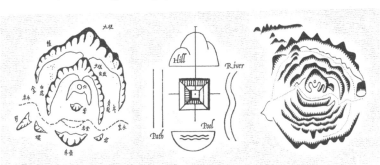

DWELLING ORIENTATION
aligning earth and heaven

Chinese geomancers identify three kinds of *Na* (receiving) *Qi* for a building: Earth *Qi*, Human *Qi*, and Heaven *Qi*. The *Sitting position*, or back wall of the house, relates to Earth, health, and relationships, and should be at a favourable orientation to the best Mountain Dragon vein. The orientation opposite is the *Facing position*, which relates to Heaven, prosperity, vitality and creative expression. The front door is best placed here, as the most important *Qi Kou* (*Qi* mouth) or portal to external environmental and Human *Qi* into a building. This face ideally has the most active view and best connection with the wider local environment, where *Sheng Qi* influences (*page 14*) are greatest.

Houses are best sited with the front garden lower than the back, with a hill or trees behind and a good *Ming Tang* and river or road in front. In mountainous areas emphasis is placed on Mountain Dragons while on plains Water Dragons are considered more important. In urban landscapes large buildings can be treated as mountains, and roads as rivers. If even one of the *Si Xiang* are well represented in the landscape, the site is auspicious, all four is excellent.

With basic orientation within the landscape established, the Luopan or Feng Shui compass is then used to fine tune the orientation of a dwelling, integrating considerations of both the Earthly *Forms School* (*pages 6-21*) and the Heavenly *Compass School* (*pages 22-37*). The Compass School developed later than the Forms School as practitioners sought more objective measurements of *Qi*, and precise degrees of direction of Forms School features are mapped using a Luopan for their *Qi* quality and effect, as we shall shortly see.

Ideal elevation

sun

descending heavenly Qi

breeze

view

back

river

xue

ascending earthly Qi

Si Xiang around a tomb

Si Xiang around a house

Si Xiang around a town

DAOIST COSMOLOGY
Chinese whispers

The Compass School of Feng Shui is founded in the root precepts of Daoist cosmology. This begins with *Wu Qi* (Nothingness), also described as *Wen Hom* (the Mystery of the Void), the source of all. *Tai Ji* is then the Great Pole from which everything hangs, depends and revolves. *Tai Ji* is perceived as existing in space at the centre of any dwelling, and as *Tian Chi* (the Heavenly Pool) in the centre of the Luopan where the magnetic needle moves. *Tian* is the universal spark, the central point or primal Heavenly force in which there is no time and space, and from which the *Four Emanations*, *Yuan*, *Heng*, *Li* and *Zhen*, then arise, creating time and space.

Yuan is the creative force, rising in the direction of *Heng* and rooted in *Zhen*. *Heng* is the ever-penetrating conscious force, which permeates and enlivens all matter. *Li* is the beneficial gathering force, the consequence of the continuation of the cycle. *Zhen* is the primal invariable and determining force; gathered from the *Qi* of *Li* it feeds the energy of *Yuan*. The text of the *Yi Jing* begins with their invocation:

"*Yuan Heng Li Zhen—the Origin, a Sacrificial Offering, Profit the Divination.*" − Yi Jing, Book of Changes [earliest written version ca. 350 BC]

The Mystery expresses itself in the *Seven Form Forces* (the *Three Gifts* plus the *Four Emanations*) as the Sun (*Yang*), Moon (*Yin*), and five Elementary planets, Mars (*Fire*), Mercury (*Water*), Jupiter (*Wood*), Venus (*Metal*) and Saturn (*Earth*). Four meditation diagrams from the *Dao Zang* Daoist Canon [ca 400 AD] are shown opposite.

*Earth - the Dark Earth of the Great Float,
the Floating Island of the Immortals.*

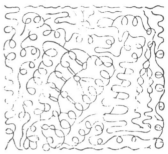

*Heaven - the Space Song of the Blue Sky, the
Sound of Jade falling from Heaven.*

*The Pattern of Change: the intercourse between
the Jade Sovereign (Heaven) and Primordial
Darkness (Earth) reveals the action of the Dao.*

*The Diagram of the Talisman - "Fu"
(Happiness) - hung to ward off bad
luck and attract good.*

HO TU AND LO SHU

the sage faces south

The *Ho Tu* describes the state of *Qi* in the spiritual plane of *Early Heaven*. A gift to Fu Xi, it appeared on the back of a Yellow River Dragon-horse in 2943 BC, and is usually written in green. The centre manifests in a vertical line, then a horizontal line, and the Elements give birth to one another in a clockwise progression moving out from the centre. The Element and trigram ascriptions of the numbers (*see page 33*) are used in surveying a site, reading a Luopan (*see page 36*) and deciding spiritual cures. Note that south is traditionally placed at the top in Chinese cosmological diagrams.

The *Lo Shu* magic square was revealed to Da Yu in 2205 BC, inscribed on the back of a tortoise which came out of the river Lo. The *Nine Palaces* provide a map of the flow of benevolent and malevolent *Qi* through time and space, on any scale, forming the basis for the numerology of *Later Heaven*, the material plane. Each sector of space is assigned a number and Element (*see pages 26-29*), and each number represents a Star of the Big Dipper constellation (*see page 54*), as well as a Trigram and its associated qualities (*see pages 30-33*). The numbers (known as "Star numbers") rotate around the *Lo Shu* in sequence to reveal changing influences in different Palaces over time (*see page 55*). The Star numbers, Elements and trigrams are used extensively in secular building and interior design.

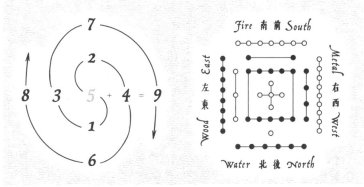

Above: The Ho Tu magic square, oriented with south at the top, the numbers creating the Elements. The first ten numbers are ascribed to the five directions and the five elements in a creation sequence with the first four numbers represent the Four Emanations (Yuan, Heng, Li and Zhen) and the next four the Five Elements, with 5 and 10 as Earth in the centre.

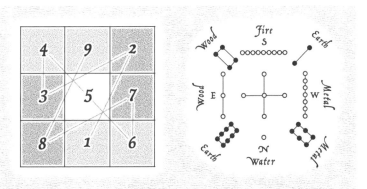

Above: The Lo Shu (magic square of Saturn). All columns, rows and diagonals add to 15. Earthly Yin even numbers form the corners, alternating with Heavenly Yang odd ones. Moving through 9 palaces (the sigil of Saturn), Qi crystallises into form and matter. Earth is central. Opposite, left to right: Ho Tu Dragon Horse; early Ho Tu; Fu Xi; Early Lo Shu; River Lo Tortoise.

FIVE ELEMENTS
creating and destroying

The *Wu Xing* or *Five Elements* of traditional Chinese cosmology are more accurately seen as phases of transformation. *Huo* Fire, *Tu* Earth, *Jin* Metal, *Shui* Water and *Mu* Wood (or Tree) are arranged in two ways, firstly as the fourfold *Early Heaven* cycle of the *Si Xiang* and *Ho Tu* with Earth in the middle (*previous page*), and secondly as the pentagonal *Later Heaven* arrangement related to the *Lo Shu* with Earth in the position of late summer (*shown opposite*).

> *"Five elements refers to water, fire, wood, metal and earth. Water is moisture below, Fire is heat rising, Wood is right and wrong, Metal is change and Earth is farming"* – Zang Zhu (Book of Burial), ascribed to Guo Po [276-324 AD].

In the *Sheng* or creative cycle (*the outer circuit opposite*) each Element creates and nourishes the next: Wood feeds Fire, Fire produces ashes of Earth, Earth yields crystalline Metal, Metal melts into Water, and Water nourishes Wood. Thus five distinct phases from birth to death are described—creation, gestation, maturation, completion and resting. Also present within the pentagram is the balancing *Ko* or control cycle. Here Fire melts Metal, Metal cuts Wood, Wood weakens Earth, Earth contains Water and Water destroys Fire.

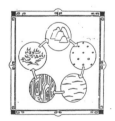  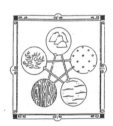

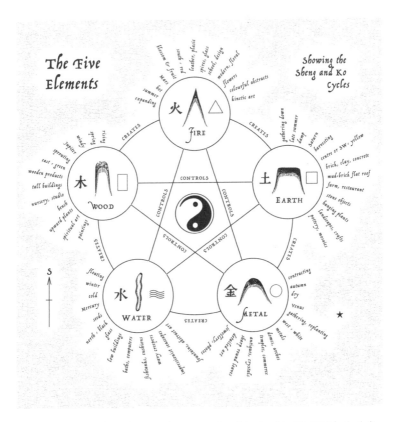

The Five Elements

Showing the Sheng and Ko Cycles

火 △ FIRE
— heat / fruit, nuts — leather, plastic — spices, glass — school, design — modern, floral — flowers — colourful abstracts — kinetic art — Mars — hot — summer — expanding

木 □ WOOD
Jupiter — windy — east = green — sprouting — wooden products — tall buildings — nursery, studio — bench — upward plants — spiritual art — paintings

土 □ EARTH
gathering down — late summer — damp — Saturn — harvesting — centre or SW, yellow — brick, clay, concrete — mud-brick flat roof — farm, restaurant — stone objects — hanging plants — landscapes, crafts — pottery, mosaics

水 〰 WATER
S ↑ — floating — winter — cold — Mercury — seeds — north, black — glass — low buildings — baths, computers — fishtanks, fountains — abstract art

金 ○ METAL
contracting — autumn — dry — Venus — gathering, replanting — metals — west, white — domes, arches — temples, commerce — ★ — antiques, round forms — crystals — jewellery, kitchens — functional, abstract art

CREATES · CREATES · CREATES · CREATES · CONTROLS · CONTROLS · CONTROLS · CONTROLS · CONTROLS

Above: The five classical Chinese Elements and assignations. In traditional medicine Wood (Mu) rules the liver, gall bladder, tendons, nerves, nails & eyes; Fire (Huo) rules the heart, pericardium, small intestine, arteries & tongue; Earth (Tu) rules the spleen, pancreas, stomach, muscles, lips & mouth; Metal (Jin) rules the lungs, large intestine, skin, body hair & nose; and Water (Shui) rules the kidneys, bladder, reproductive organs, bones & ears. The five Emotions are assigned as Joy-Fire, Worry-Earth, Grief-Metal, Fear-Water & Anger-Wood; and the five notes in the Pentatonic Scale Do-Earth, Re-Metal, Mi-Wood, So-Fire & La-Water, as are moves in martial arts, strokes in calligraphy, etc. Opposite: Sheng Cycle; Birth of five Elements; Ko Cycle.

27

ELEMENTS IN THE LANDSCAPE
nourishing and clashing patterns

The presence of two or more Elements in a situation creates various dynamic patterns. Similar Elements (e.g. an Earth structure in an Earth environment) will be mutually supportive, while elements with others preceding or following them in the *Sheng* cycle will be harmonious (so, for example, it is considered very auspicious to have three mountain peaks around a site shaped to suggest Wood, Fire and Earth). Likewise, a Water building in a Wood environment will drain itself to benefit the community, and a commercial building with a triangular Fire motif will be nourished by, and therefore drain, the Wood forms of neighbouring rectangular buildings. However, when Elements are present with others preceding or following them on the *Ko* cycle, clashing disharmonious *Qi* is created, so a Wood building in a Metal environment will be oppressed, while an Earth building in a Water one will bring business success at the expense of respect.

When a structure is affected by an Element that is harmful to it, or is of mixed Elements, a harmonising or controlling Element may be introduced using shape, colour, substance or symbol at an appropriate scale. Thus for a Metal Element threatening a Wood house, Water will drain the Metal and nourish the Wood on the *Sheng* cycle (e.g. a water feature). As another example, a Metal house in a Fire environment will benefit from the introduction of Water (to control Fire) and Earth (to drain Fire and nourish Metal), possibly using a rockery and pond.

You can use the diagram on the previous page to help find imaginative solutions to rebalancing the elements around you.

THE WHITE TIGER
BEARS THE FIVE
ELEMENTS (CENTRE).
CLOCKWISE FROM TOP:
THE SHARP ANGLES
OF FIRE; THE FLAT
PLAINS OF EARTH;
THE ROUNDED SHAPES
OF METAL; THE
FLOWING LINES OF
WATER; TOWERING
FORMS OF WOOD.

BA GUA
the eight trigrams

As *Yin* and *Yang* generate the *Si Xiang*, so each of the four Celestial Spirits further divide into a son and daughter to create the *Ba Gua* or eight *trigrams* (*below left*). *Shao Yang* ⚎ gives rise to *Zhen* ☳ and *Li* ☲, *Tai Yang* ⚌ to *Dui* ☱ and *Qian* ☰, *Shao Yin* ⚍ to *Xun* ☴ and *Kan* ☵, and *Tai Yin* ⚏ to *Gen* ☶ and *Kun* ☷.

While the origins of the names for the eight trigrams are lost in history (although they hint at a possible pan-Celtic derivation) their meanings are derived from the images they suggest (*opposite*). In accordance with the Three Gifts (*see page 4*) the top line of a trigram relates to Heaven and the future, the middle line to Humankind and the present, and the bottom line to Earth and the past.

As we shall see on the next page, both the positions of the eight trigrams in the *Early* and *Later Heaven* wheels and their Elemental assignations are related to the *Ho Tu* and *Lo Shu* magic squares. The external environment of a house is read primarily in the *Early Heaven Ba Gua*, while the internal environment in the *Later Heaven Ba Gua*, each shining through and balancing the other.

Qian (chien) is HEAVEN, its three solid Yang lines symbolising the essential spirit from which all else is manifest; strength, power, creativity, authority, time, duration, immaterial.

Kun is EARTH, its three broken Yin lines open to receive heaven's blessings as the soil receives nourishment from the sun and rain; yielding, receptive, passivity, surrender, space, extension, material.

Zhen (chen) is THUNDER, the trigram shows a solid powerful rising force, dispersing harmlessly; arousing, movement, activity, growth, natural shock, exciting, impetus, stimulation, volition, impulse, vitality.

Xun (Sun) is WIND, which has no root but carries a powerful force over the ground; small efforts, gentle effects, work, flexibility, penetrating, sensitivity, responsivity, intuition, assimilation, pervasiveness.

Kan is WATER, which appears clear and open, but has substance in the middle; mysterious, profound, meaningful, dangerous, difficult, dark, formless, uncertainty, emotion, Eros, Lunar forces.

Li is FIRE, the image of a flame, with solid form on the outside but empty in the middle; illuminating, intelligence, dependence, attachment, bright, formed, clarity, discrimination, Logos, Solar forces.

Gen (Ken) is MOUNTAIN, the image of space in a container, a solid surface pushed up by the earth below; stillness, resting, meditation, equanimity, solidity, immobility, heaviness, concentration.

Dui (Tui) is LAKE, the trigram open on the surface with mass below, like a body of water reflecting the Moon; openness, pleasure, satisfaction, excess, buoyancy, lightness, joyful, observation, intuitive vision, volatility.

Fu Xi & Wang Wen Ba Gua

early and late heaven arrangements

The *Fu Xi* or *Xian Tian* (*Early Heaven*) arrangement (*upper opposite*) of the *Ba Gua* derives from the *Ho Tu* (*see page 24*), with opposite trigrams facing across the centre. Heaven balances firm yielding Earth, gentle Wind balances arousing Thunder, mysterious Water balances illuminating Fire; still Mountain balances joyful Lake. This sequence depicts the timeless Heavenly order and is emphasised in outdoor, temple and tomb designs, locating form, function and symbol in space and time, and for diagnosing problems.

The more widely used *Wen Wang* or *Hou Tian* (*Later Heaven*) *Ba Gua* sequence (*lower opposite*) describes the practical application of the trigrams to Earth *Qi* via the cycle of seasons. It is emphasised in residential and commercial design. The Nine Palaces of the *Lo Shu* ascribe the trigrams to eight directions on any scale (city, house or room), indicating the best rooms for specific functions or family members and the spiritual health of the household, with the central Palace as the *Tai Ji*, the vertical axis between Heaven and Earth.

Ba Gua directions from the centre of the house indicate problems and remedies, e.g. a *Sha* form (*see page 42*) to the south augurs headaches and authority problems, particularly for the father (*Early Heaven Qian*), and eye and reputation (fame) problems, especially for the middle daughter (*Later Heaven Li*). Doorways, extensions, windows, mirrors, talismans, plant and animal symbols, *Lo Shu* numbers and Five Element cures such as pictures, colour, and ornaments can be used to enhance or remedy *Ba Gua* directions. A useful skill here is to notice metaphors suggested by forms and images around you.

Early Heaven Fu Xi Ba Gua (top left diagram):

father · S 1 · grandfather
head + central nervous
eldest · SW 5 · daughter
hips + respiratory

youngest · SE 2 · daughter
mouth + endocrine

CREATIVE
HEAVEN — Qian 乾
PERSISTENT
WIND — Xun 巽

JOYFUL
LAKE — Dui 兌

middle · W 6 · son
ears + urogenital

PERILOUS
WATER — Kan 坎

middle · E 3 · daughter
eyes + cardiovascular

CLINGING
FIRE — Li 離

STILL
MOUNTAIN — Gen 艮

AROUSING
THUNDER — Kun 坤

youngest · NW 7 · son
hands + skeletal

RECEPTIVE
EARTH

eldest · NE 4 · son
feet + motor sensory

mother · N 8 · grandmother
digestive + reproductive

Left and above: The sacred Early Heaven Fu Xi Ba Gua: The universe is revealed as the wheel rotates. "Heaven and Earth anchor the positions. Vapour flows between mountain and lake. Thunder and wind nourish each other. Fire and water do not conflict" (Yi Jing).

Right: The secular Later Heaven Wang Wen Ba Gua (outwardly facing version above): Two duck figures (conjugal bliss) in the SW of a house or room will enhance relationships. A water feature (feeds Wood) southeast aids prosperity.

Later Heaven Wang Wen Ba Gua (bottom right diagram):

noon · S 9 · lounge
summer solstice

Human Gate
afternoon · SW 2 · dining rm
lammas

FAME
FIRE — Li 離

Earth Gate
morning · SE 4 · kitchen
beltane

PROSPERITY
SMALL WOOD — Xun 巽

RELATIONSHIPS
BIG EARTH — Kun 坤

CREATIVITY
SMALL METAL — Dui 兌

dawn · E 3 · morning rm
spring equinox

HEALTH
BIG WOOD — Zhen 震

BENEFACTORS
BIG METAL — Qian 乾

sunset · W 7 · playroom
autumn equinox

KNOWLEDGE
SMALL EARTH — Gen 艮

CAREER JOURNEY
WATER — Kan 坎

Heaven Gate
evening · NW 6 · office
samhain

night · NE 8 · infolk
imbolc

bathroom
midnight · N 1 · winter solstice

YI JING
the book of changes

According to tradition it was Zhou Wen Wang (King Wen) who first combined the *Ba Gua* to form and name the sixty-four hexagrams in the *Gua Ci* [c.1142 BC], in the early days of the Zhou dynasty. One of his sons, Zhou Gong Dan, later wrote the *Yao Ci*, a commentary on each of the lines, 384 in all (also the number of days in 13 moons).

The *Zhou Yi Jing* is used in both *Early* and *Later Heaven* sequences, and both can appear on a *Luopan* compass (*see page 36*). Site, building and door orientations are traditionally interpreted according to the hexagram and *Yao* (line) located in the respective compass direction from the centre of the property or doorway. Auspicious or inauspicious omens are then discovered in the text of the *Yi Jing*, the meaning of each *Gua* (symbol) being derived from the attributes and relationships of its two component trigrams (*see pages 56-57*). Specific Hexagrams can define plan and elevation in palace, building and garden design

The oracle may also be consulted by a ritual sequence of either dividing yarrow stalks or casting coins, in order to gain insight into questions of location and timing. Building the hexagram from the bottom, for each line three coins can be thrown, one or three heads indicating an unbroken *Yang* line, one or three tails a broken *Yin* line.

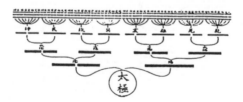

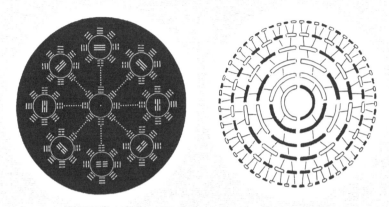

Above left: The sixty four hexagrams are each built from two Ba Gua trigrams.
Right: The evolution of Tai Ji to Yin Yang, Si Xiang, Ba Gua and the hexagrams.

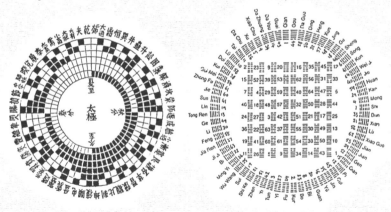

Above left: A similar scheme to above top right: Above right: The positions of the sixty-four Gua in Heaven (circle) and on Earth (square), with 1 Qian due south at the top.

THE LUOPAN
the geomancer's compass

Luo means all-encompassing net, *Pan* means plate, and the first known Luopan or Feng Shui compass with directional characters (*centre-left below*) dates to the Warring States Period [475-221 BC].

A modern Luopan consists of a rotating circular plate set in a square base overlaid with sighting crosshairs. The device is placed carefully, level and raised, at the *Tian Xin,* Heavenly Heart, or centre of a building or site with the base aligned to the walls (*below left*). The disk is rotated until the magnetic needle aligns with the line and dots in the central *Tian Qi* or Heaven Pool (*see opposite top*). Bearings to interior and surrounding features such as doorways, windows, gates, garden features, mountains, roads and waterways are then judged by characteristics read off appropriate rings on the rotated plate (*pages 50-57*). For example, the *Ho Tu* ordered trigrams of the Early Heaven *Ba Gua* (*the ring around the compass in both diagrams opposite*) might be applied to external features, and the *Lo Shu* glyphs of the Later Heaven *Ba Gua* (*the next ring out lower opposite*) to interior design. For example, a house sitting in (with its back to) the northeast is in Early Heaven *Zhen Gua*, Later Heaven *Gen Gua* (*Lo Shu* Star 8), and faces southwest, Early Heaven *Xun Gua*, Later Heaven *Kun Gua* (*Lo Shu* Star 2).

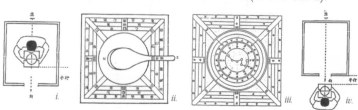

Left: San He (Triple Harmony) Luopan, emphasising three different 24 Mountain rings (Earth plate for Ba Gua, Mountain Dragons and facing/sitting axis, Human plate for footstool hills and local built environment, and Heaven plate for reading Water Dragons and stars). The outer two plates are rotated by 7.5° in each direction, reflecting the notion that Human Qi comes after Earth Qi, while faster Heaven Qi arrives early. See pages 52-53.

Right: San Yuan (Triple Era) Luopan, emphasising Nine Star and Yi Jing rings (see 54 and 53). The Nine Stars refer both to the nine stars of the Big Dipper (Plough) and the Nine Palaces of the Lo Shu (see page 25). Also shown are the 64 hexagrams of the Yi Jing (pages 56-57). Most rings detailing Daoist and Confucian calendrical and metaphysical cycles were added after the Tang dynasty [618-907 AD].

Opposite: i. How to read a Luopan from a dwelling's centre. ii. The Si Nan Luopan (c. 300 BC) with its fabled lodestone spoon (now thought to be an archaeological error). The square bronze divination plate shows the 8 Trigrams, 10 Stems, 12 Branches and 28 Lunar Mansions. iii. Han dynasty (206 BC-220 AD) Liu Ren divination plate. iv. How to read a Luopan for door orientation.

37

UNDERGROUND ENERGIES
subterranean Water Dragons

According to classical Feng Shui, various manmade and landscape features can cause troubling geopathic stress problems for a site. The Ming Dynasty [1368-1644] text *Shui Peng Ba Zhen Fa* (*Eight Needles of the Water Compass Method*) gives a protocol for divining underground streams, cavities, geological faults, mineral deposits, old wells, tombs, abattoirs and battlefields. An even earlier text states:

> *"In the subterranean regions there are alternate layers of earth and rock and flowing spring waters. These strata rest upon thousands of vapours (Qi) which are distributed in tens of thousands of branches, veins and threadlike openings...The body of the earth is like that of a human being..." (Chen Su Xiao d.1332).*

Underground meridians are regularly disturbed by excavations for building foundations, quarries, mines, and embankments and cuttings for roads and railways, and in China offerings are traditionally made to the local landscape spirits before such works are undertaken. Traumatic blockage of *Long Mai* and the resulting stagnation in the flows of *Qi* generally give rise to toxic *Sha Qi*, poisonous energy which rises especially from underground water meridians. This can have major health implications for those living directly above.

Ideally places with such influences should be avoided or designed to minimise their effects. Alternatively, protective charms may be used to shield a residence, or *Earth Acupuncture* can be employed to release landscape trauma and restore the healthy flow of *Qi* to injured underground Water Dragons. This may involve the temporary or permanent insertion of wood, metal or stone needles into nodes on the meridian pathways to heal and harmonise the disturbed *Qi*.

Above: Pagodas, like huge acupuncture needles, may be sited to control dangerous visible and underground Water Dragons. Regular ceremonies also maintain the spiritual hygiene of an area.

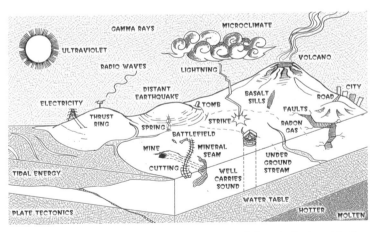

Above: Choosing the exact place to site a house or town is not only determined by determining the healthy Sheng Qi, but also by avoiding the hidden and visible geopathic factors which cause Sha Qi.

SHA QI
hostile forces, causes and cures

The term *Sha*, literally 'poison', covers a range of hostile environmental influences. Straight lines such as roads, fences, power cables or sharp corners that point at a dwelling are considered unfortunate, as they aim *Sha Qi* towards the front door and can carry malevolent spirits. The only straight lines found in the classical landscape are leys incorporated into temple and palace design, with a series of gatehouse pagodas to step down and cleanse the *Qi* as it approaches the site. Roads and paths, like most natural forms, are best when curving and meandering. The outsides of bends in rivers and roads, T-junctions, forks, and the entrances to valleys, wind tunnels between buildings and bridgeheads are all considered dangerous and therefore inauspicious, as are ugly or threatening local features, especially if facing the front door or main room.

Feng Shui solutions may be *Ru Shi*, physical changes (*e.g. see lower opposite*) including moving the location or orientation of a door, or they can be *Chu Shi*, psychological and transcendental changes, such as installing a mirror, animal symbol or talisman. Shown below (*left*) is a *Sha*-averting stone facing a bridge. The stone which blocks the *Sha* is inscribed *Shi Gan Tang*—'the stone dares to resist'.

Left: Taoist temple design harnessing the Heavenly Qi of a ley line. Centre: The talismanic Door Gods Shen Du and Yu Lie are often placed to guard the portal against demons especially from the potentially dangerous northeast. Right: Seeking to avoid Sha Qi altogether.

Left: Nasty Sha Qi. Right: Cures include removal of the threatening feature, protective walls and vegetation, a concave or Ba Gua mirror to deflect, a fountain or pond to absorb, a pair of guardian stone lions at the portal, and a round object ('completeness') in front of the house.

HOUSE AND PLOT SHAPES
living in squares and triangles

Many dwellings in China have a circular pond within a rectangular courtyard, or a circular door in the garden (*see page 46-7*), thus creating a union of the Heavenly circle and the Earthly square. The ideal plot shape is square (representing the Earth element which supports humans) or rectangular (representing the Wood element which supports growth), oriented with the sides facing the cardinal directions. The dwelling should have the same orientation and be located in the centre, with the same precepts regarding plot shape applying also to house and room shape. Missing corners suggest *Ba Gua* shortcomings and will direct *Sha Qi* towards the dwelling from the internal corner.

Triangular plots (representing the Fire element) are inauspicious as the sharp corners tend to trap stagnant *Qi,* yielding thick *Predecessor Qi*, the presence of the past in the atmosphere of place, a vibrational imprint of previous activities and inhabitants, which may include *Gui* or spirits. Irregular plots belong to the Water element (which supports Wood) and can be good or bad depending on the shape. They are to be avoided if the form and slope direct *Qi* away from the building, or if areas of the house stagnate outside the flow of *Qi*.

Cures for sick shapes often involve introducing landscape enhancements to represent the elements of missing trigrams, or by creating separate well-shaped garden areas within the whole. Terracing can help contain the *Qi* on steep slopes, especially if the back of the plot is lower than the front, in which case the house might well be better reoriented with the main door facing downhill.

Above: Roof profiles are uplifted to invoke Heaven. Corners and ridges may display sculptures of protective magical animals, such as the Chinese Dragon, which has elements of nine different animals.

Above: Inauspicious (left and centre) and auspicious (right) plot and house shapes. Missing areas can be rectified with an extension, or improved with a tree, light or mirrors (lowest row).

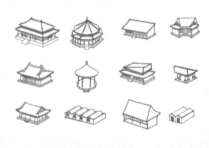

Above: Auspicious (left) and inauspicious (right) roofs. Pointed and wedge shaped profiles and Sha creating eave and gutter forms are avoided.

Left: A classical northern Chinese house with an internal Ming Tang (see page 12) courtyard—an ideal model for maximising healthy Sheng Qi.

43

INTERIOR DESIGN PRECEPTS
containment and flow

The entrance to a house is like its mouth, leading to the business and public living areas, while the kitchen and family living areas are its heart and the bedrooms and bathrooms the private parts. The design of a house should reflect this progression from public to private space, with a clearly defined frontage, the front door not opening directly onto the kitchen, stairs or toilet. The placement of doors, windows and furniture should allow the flow of *Qi* to meander and circulate, avoiding long straight lines. If the front and back doors or gates are in a straight line, or the windows in the main rooms opposite each other, the *Qi* will leak and prosperity will not congregate.

Beds, desks and sofas should be arranged following the principles of *Si Xiang* (*see page 16*) to provide a sense of enclosure. Bathrooms and toilets should never be in the central *Tai Ji* area, nor over the front door or stove. Partially offset doors can generate irritability, while irregular plans often create *Scattered Qi* and pockets of *Sha*, which can be cured with round objects, e.g. rugs or tables. *Cutting Qi* from sharp internal corners can be masked with plants or fabric, and *Oppressive Qi* from beams lightened with corbels, flutes, feathers or a canopy. Mirrors raise *Yang Qi,* expand space, amplify whatever they reflect, but impair sleep overlighting a bed.

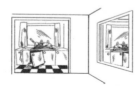

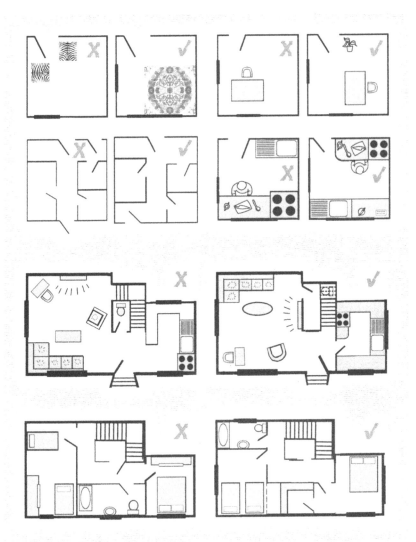

CLASSICAL GARDEN DESIGN
heaven on earth

Classical Chinese garden design is rooted in *Yin Yang* theory, as a crafted harmony of Earth and Heaven, the dots in the *Tai Ji* symbol suggesting the inclusion of the sky within the design, smaller gardens within bigger gardens, and the impression of unlimited space within a compact space. Compositions balance naturalistic landscaping with symmetrical buildings, using hills and rockeries, watercourses and ponds, bridges and corridors, pavilions and paths, walls and lattice windows, trees and shrubs, lawns and flowers, ornaments and poetic calligraphy, birdsong and music, animal life and human ceremony.

Circles and curves suggest Heaven, and squares and straight lines Earth. A square lawn can be combined with a circular entrance door (a moon gate), or a circular pavilion placed near a square pond.

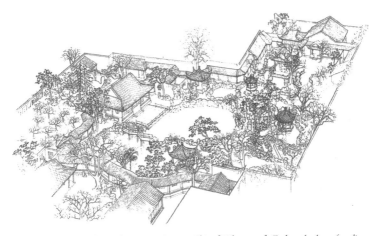

Above: Happy Garden, Suzhou, Jiangsu Province, China [19th century]. Each garden has a founding theme and one climax feature. We walk and stand seeing a series of views, from differing elevations, some framed by pavilions, some borrowed from outside the garden, avoiding a full view of the whole garden at once, until we reach the focus and then depart through increasingly serene vistas.

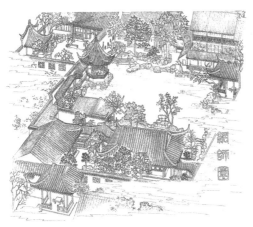

Left: Retired Fisherman's Garden, Suzhou, Jiangsu province, China [built 1140, rebuilt c.1750]. It combines movement within stillness, substantial within insubstantial, with symbolisms suggested by plants and simulacra and juxtapositions of design raising ambiguities and insights. Both Early and Later Heaven Ba Gua directions influence garden design. Opposite: Rockery garden within Lingering Here Garden, also Suzhou [built 1593]

APPENDIX I – DESIGN OF BEIJING

Like the importance of the head to a Dragon, the Feng Shui of the capital (and within that the design of the Imperial Palace or President's residence) affects the fortunes of the entire country—the capital is also the metaphorical centre of the universe. Beijing is located at the head of the northern Mountain Dragon Range, the Qi flowing from the northern and western hills to the city, a microcosmic metaphor for the topography of China. The site was chosen because of its resemblance to the "Regal Throne" located near the celestial North Pole, the surrounding mountain ranges providing a reflection of the stars of the Zi Wei constellation. The Heavenly Emperor resides at the Zi Wei star, while the surrounding stars form the Imperial Court of Heaven, representing the Empress, Concubines, Princes, Lords and Mandarins. Ancient Chinese cosmology regards all earthly forms such as countries, cities and even individual beings as reflections of the celestial stars in heaven.

Tai Wo Palace, the seat of the Imperial Throne and the most important building in Beijing, is oriented on the four cardinal points determined by the four altars of the Sun, Moon, Earth and Heaven. These are laid out following the Former Heaven Ba Gua—the altar of Heaven to the south, Earth to the north, Sun to the east, and Moon to the west. Other altars to the gods of land and grain, agriculture, hills and rivers, and silkworms, are located along the main axes. The Eight Altars, whose

purpose were timely offerings to spirits to bring peace and harmony to the capital and the entire country, form the principal metaphysical design elements in the planning of Beijing.

In order to increase the good Heavenly *Yang* Qi flowing from the Mountain Dragon range in the north-west into the city, pagodas and towers were built to the north-west and west of Beijing to direct the Qi to the Imperial Palace, starting from the sacred spring on Uchun Shan from which the Emperor obtained his drinking water. The only structures that are higher than the Tai Wo Palace are the Coal Hill Pavilion at the back of the palace to the north, and the Buddhist stupa and temple of Yamataka. Yamataka is the spiritual protector of Beijing and the White Pagoda stupa gives blessing and protection to the Emperor from the northwestern and northern heights.

Ming and Qing dynasty Beijing was laid out according to the Early and Later Heaven Ba Gua and the interaction of the Five Elements, and provides an excellent example of Chinese metaphysics in application.

SOUTH represents the Fire element, the metaphor for technology, civilization and progress, and here is found the main city gate by which the Emperor rules and brings prosperity and progress to the country.

NORTH represents Water, money and wealth: a Drum Tower and Bell Tower are located to the north of

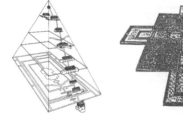

the Imperial Palace. Formerly the bell was rung in the morning to herald the opening of the city gates and the drum was struck in the evening to herald their closing. The bell belongs to the Metal element, which gives rise to the Water of the North and ensures the healthy development of the state treasury; the drum belongs to the Earth element, controlling and sealing the prosperity.

EAST represents the Wood element, growth and prosperity, and in the original design a forest was planted just outside the East Gate to enrich the Wood of the East.

WEST represents the Metal element, war, disputes, and other bad omens: there are three lakes to the West of the Imperial Palace, which reduce the harmful effects of the Metal element of the West, as Metal feeds Water. The two main Stars representing the Emperor also reside in the West: a twin pagoda temple is built to the West of Tien An Men to denote them. An early hill form, now Bu Bu Shan Cemetery is also located in the West: Earth gives rise to Metal—weakening and rebuilding

Metal by Feng Shui allows the Metal element to be used as a tool by humanity.

NORTHEAST denotes the trigram *Gen*, symbolising young men: the temple of Confucius and the State University are located in this corner.

SOUTHEAST denotes the trigram *Xun* and symbolises intellectual fame and literature, which is increased by the Wen Chang Pagoda; here is found an area of lakes and marshes, now public gardens, the Water element of the lakes nourishing the Wood element of the Southeast.

SOUTHWEST denotes the trigram *Kun*, the people, flat land—this corner of the city was mainly residential cottages and flat land, and the Gate of Humans through which the Emperor travelled out of Beijing to visit the country.

NORTHWEST represents the trigram *Qian*, Gods, Buddha and the ancestors: the high pagodas and temples are mainly located in this direction, while the North Lake here reduces the harmful effect of the Metal element of the Northwest.

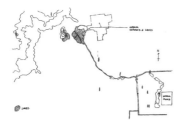

APPENDIX II – THE 10 STEMS

The ten Heavenly Stems 'contain water', and 'reflect the Milky Way'. Their (24 Mountain) directions are 'opened' by the siting of gateways, doors, windows, views, water-course entry and exits, roads and paths.

Stems 3, 4, 7 & 8 are 'Lucky', linked with *Gen* and *Xun Gua* which have mixed *Yin* and *Yang* and so are fertile.

Stems 1, 2, 9 & 10 are 'Unlucky', linked with *Qian* and *Kun Gua* which are overwhelmingly *Yang* or *Yin* respectively.

Stems 5 & 6 are central, the 'Tortoise Shell', or middle of the universe; they are used to control the dispersal of *Sha*.

1. *Jia* 甲 depicts a shell or bud, hard and enclosing, a fingernail or guard's helmet, protecting what is precious.

2. Yi 乙 is a sprout appearing out of the mother plant, the expression of creativity.

3. *Bing* 丙 represents the fire in the hearth of the house.

4. *Ding* 丁 is a hammered-in nail, the penetrating power of Heaven, virile, potent, able to stand on its own.

5. *Wu* 戊 is a scythe, cutting and reaping.

6. *Ji* 己 is sorting, the warp and weft of weaving.

7. *Geng* 庚 is winnowing, the hard work of getting the precious grain out of the husk.

8. *Xin* 辛 is accurate and bitter, offending superiors, punishment and fear, the bite of the tiger.

9. *Ren* 壬 is a servant shouldering a pole with two water buckets, bearing the burden, supporting life, child bearing.

10. *Gui* 癸 is a bow bent with arrows ready to fly, a secret movement of waters, the fertility of life in sperm and ovum.

APPENDIX III – THE 12 BRANCHES

The 12 EARTHLY BRANCHES mark the 12 terrestrial compass directions and the location of Earthly Dragon *Qi*. They also indicate the 12-double hour divisions of a day, months in a year, and years of Jupiter's solar orbit. The year begins at Winter Solstice, midway through Branch 1 (due north), the rest of the branches relating compass directions to moments in time. The branches also indicate best directions relative to a person's birth year, and the best times of the year for initiating projects connected with building or burying.

The *Xia Li* (*Thousand Year*) calendar describes time (years, months, days and double-hours) in recurring cycles of sixty Stem and Branch combinations, also found in the 60, 72, 120 and 240 direction Dragon rings on some Luopans.

1. *Zi* 子 is a baby wrapped in swaddling clothes, Winter Solstice, gate of death and life, hidden power of *Yang* in *Yin*.

2. *Chou* 丑 is a young plant supported by a stick. Binding to help growth at the beginning.

3. *Yin* 寅 is hands joining in greeting and reverence.

4. *Mao* 卯 is a pair of doors opening, the rising sun, Spring Equinox, the power of Wood and the *Qing* Dragon.

5. *Chen* 辰 is a woman with hiding her belly, pregnant and timid, movement in a Spring egg.

6. *Si* 巳 is a fully-grown foetus, and fruits forming.

7. *Wu* 午 is opposition, the strong vertical power from Heaven, Summer Solstice, the heat of fire at its zenith.

8. *Wei* 未 is the roots and stem of a tree heavily laden with fruit, the power of Heaven coming to the Earth.

9. *Shen* 申 represents two hands holding a rope between them, expanding power, connection to the Spirits.

10. *You* 酉 is a liquor fermenting in a jug, distillation, harvest, Autumn Equinox, Heaven coming into Earth.

11. *Xu* 戌 is a scythe, weapon, injuring or killing, cutting what is unnecessary, clearing the ground before sowing.

12. *Hai* 亥 is a man and woman making love, *Yin* and *Yang* combining under a roof to conceive.

APPENDIX IV – THE 60 JIA ZI

THE 10 HEAVENLY STEMS

No.	Ch.	Nam.	Yn/g	Nature	Elmnt	Season
1	甲	Jia	○	Adaptable	Wood	Spring
2	乙	Yi	●	Flexible	Wood	Spring
3	丙	Bing	○	Generous	Fire	Summer
4	丁	Ding	●	Leader	Fire	Summer
5	戊	Wu	○	Loyal	Earth	Centre
6	己	Ji	●	Nurturing	Earth	Centre
7	庚	Geng	○	Stamina	Metal	Autumn
8	辛	Xin	●	Attention	Metal	Autumn
9	壬	Ren	○	Moving	Water	Winter
10	癸	Gui	●	Still	Water	Winter

THE 12 EARTHLY BRANCHES

No.	Ch.	Month	Yn/g	Anim.	Nature	Elmnt
I	子	Zi	○	Rat	Quick-witted	Water
II	丑	Chou	●	Ox	Steadfast	Earth
III	寅	Yin	○	Tiger	Authoritative	Wood
IV	卯	Mao	●	Rabbit/Hare	Homely	Wood
V	辰	Chen	○	Dragon	Charismatic	Earth
VI	巳	Si	●	Snake	Seductive	Fire
VII	午	Wu	○	Horse	Free	Fire
VIII	未	Wei	●	Sheep/Goat	Creative	Earth
IX	申	Shen	○	Monkey	Fun-loving	Metal
X	酉	You	●	Rooster	Practical	Metal
XI	戌	Xu	○	Dog	Faithful	Earth
XII	亥	Hai	●	Pig/Boar	Perfectionist	Water

THE 60 JIA ZI - STEMS AND BRANCHES

Stem	1 Jia	2 Yi	3 Bing	4 Ding	5 Wu	6 Ji	7 Geng	8 Xin	9 Ren	10 Gui
Branch										
I Zi	1924 1984		1936 1996		1948 2008		1960 2020		1972 2032	
II Chou		1925 1985		1937 1997		1949 2009		1961 1921		1973 2033
III Yin	1974 2034		1926 1986		1938 1998		1950 2010		1962 1922	
IV Mao		1975 2035		1927 1987		1939 1999		1951 2011		1963 1923
V Chen	1964 2024		1976 2036		1928 1988		1940 2000		1952 2012	
VI Si		1965 2025		1977 2037		1929 1989		1941 2001		1953 2013
VII Wu	1954 2014		1966 2026		1978 2038		1930 1990		1942 2002	
VIII Wei		1955 2015		1967 2027		1979 2039		1931 1991		1943 2003
IX Shen	1944 2004		1956 2016		1968 2028		1980 2040		1932 1992	
X You		1945 2005		1957 2017		1969 2029		1981 2041		1933 1993
XI Xu	1934 1994		1946 2006		1958 2018		1970 2030		1982 2042	
XII Hai		1935 1995		1947 2007		1959 2019		1971 2031		1983 2043

Left: The 60 JIA ZI are composed of same-polarity combinations of the 10 Stems and 12 Branches. Years, months, days and double-hours are represented as recurring cycles of alternating Yang and Yin, always following the same diagonal sequence as shown. Use the table to find the Stem and Branch for your year of birth and then refer to the tables above..

Below: Earthly Branches appear as four Element triangles, each composed of Three Stages: Sheng (birth), Wang (growth) and Mu (death), the San He or Triple Harmony, shown (below left) with the Liu He Harmonic Combination. The best branches to locate a front door, stove, bedroom and altar are those which harmonise with your birth year. Avoid the Zhong Sha or Direct Kill and its two related branches, and the Liu Sha Antipathy (below right).

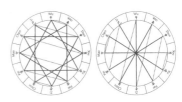

APPENDIX V – 24 MOUNTAINS

THE TWENTY-FOUR MOUNTAIN directions of the Luopan were created during the Tang dynasty using the magnetic north-south axis as the frame of reference, called the *Correct Needle of the Earth Plate*, or *Di Pan*. The twelve Branches alternate every 30° around the compass with eight of the ten Stems (omitting the earth pair) and the four corner *Ba Gua* trigrams from the *Later Heaven Ba Gua*. Study the example on the facing page.

The four *Gua* in their corner Mountain positions represent spirit doorways, all potentially inauspicious with reference to water-course directions and gateway placement. For Stems and Branches lookup tables refer to the appendices on the previous page. Here are the four *Gua* Mountains:

Gen ☶, Mountain, NE, is *Yin* power, the womb conceiving and giving birth. Dawn, the Chinese New Year *Li Chun*, Celtic Imbolc. The Feast of St. Brigid, Goddess of the Hearth.

Xun ☴, Wind, the SE Mountain, is the invisible power of Heaven which stirs everything into motion, Beltane, the weaving of colours around the Maypole.

Kun ☷, Earth, the SW Mountain, is the abundant mother, bountiful and fruitful, giving on all three *Yao*, Celtic Lughnasad, the Festival of the Goddess of Grain.

Qian ☰, Heaven, the NW Mountain, is the *Yang* power going deep into *Yin* in order to be protected, corresponding to Samhain, the release of Spirit from form.

The *San He* Luopan contains three identical yet rotated 24 Mountain rings, each with several supporting rings.

The inner *Earth Plate* has *Wu* aligned to magnetic south and reveals whether a particular directional influence is effective principally on the spiritual, mental and emotional plane (Stems), material and social plane (Branches), or mediating and stabilising plane (*Gua*). It is used to establish direction and orientation, to determine where a tomb or house 'sits' and 'faces', and to judge the quality of Earth *Qi* in the Mountain Dragon veins influencing the site. The *Sitting Direction* is the direction from the centre to back of the site

and the *Facing Direction* that from the centre to the front of the site. The Sitting and Facing Mountains are ideally both *Yin* or *Yang*, with the axis of orientation not too close to the unstable *Qi* of a border. The ring is also useful for the placement of features in a design as it can be used to activate particular quality of Qi.

The intermediate *Central Needle of the Human Plate* ring, the *Ren Pan*, is rotated 7.5° anticlockwise from the Earth Plate and was added in the Tang Dynasty. It is used to judge the quality of the small hills (called "Sand" or "Sha") in front of the *Xue*, as well as local hills and large rocks, trees and outbuildings, using the Five Elements..

The outer *Seam Needle of the Heaven Plate* ring, the *Tian Pan*, was added during the Southern Song Dynasty. It is rotated 7.5° clockwise from the Earth Plate, and is used to assess water flows, including wells, driveways and roads, and grasp good water and wealth. Water is auspicious if flowing from a vigorous direction, or to an unfavourable direction, but inauspicious towards a vigorous direction.

Above: Tang Dynasty [618-907AD] bronze astrological mirror showing the 4 Spirits, 8 Trigrams, 12 Animals representing the Branches, 24 Mountains and 28 Lunar Mansions.

APPENDIX VI – EXAMPLE LUOPAN

Rings, reading out from the centre:

1. *Heaven Pool with needle*
2. *Early Heaven Ba Gua*
3. *Lo Shu 9 Stars*
4. *8 Evil Yellow Springs*
5. *Yin Yang*

6. *Earth Plate 24 Mountains*
7. *Human Plate 24 Mountains*
8. *Heaven Plate 24 Mountains*
9. *64 Yi Jing*
10. *Degrees*

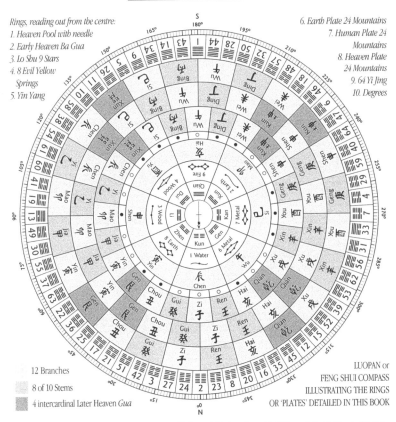

12 Branches
8 of 10 Stems
4 intercardinal Later Heaven *Gua*

LUOPAN or
FENG SHUI COMPASS
ILLUSTRATING THE RINGS
OR 'PLATES' DETAILED IN THIS BOOK

The Eight Evils Yellow Spring plate is used to establish inauspicious directions of water coming towards a dwelling. It relates to visible moving water such as rivers, and paths, gates and doorways. The *Lo Shu* direction of the Sitting position yields the unfavourable 24 Mountain Earthly Branch direction, e.g. a 9 (south) sitting house has unfavourable water in the *Hai* 24 Mountain Earth Plate direction. This can be remedied by screening the view or altering the door angle.

APPENDIX VII – JIU XING, 9 STARS

THE NINE STARS of the *Bei Dou* (Big Dipper) constellation are linked with the Nine Palaces of the *Lo Shu*. The Chinese calendar is based on a 180-year cycle, divided into three 60-year *Yuan*. Each Yuan is further divided into three 20-year *Yun* each of which relates to a number 1-9 and a *Gua* (*see table below*). Each year also has a ruling star whose number 1-9 is found by counting backwards where 2013 is 5, 2014 is 4, 2015 is 3, 2016 is 2, 2017 is 1 etc. Construct a Flying Star chart by placing the ruling star number of the current year, *Yun*, or *Yuan* of a building's construction in the centre and flying the stars forward through the 9 Palaces according to the *Lo Shu* sequence. Or choose one of the nine opposite which has the required central ruling Star number.

In the San Yuan tradition, if the centre number is for example 8, the lucky *Zhen Shen* (Original Spirit) and best Mountain position is in the NE (as in the *Lo Shu*); the weaker *Ling Shen* (Fragmentary Spirit) and best Water position is opposite in the SW; and the *Zhao Shen* (Illuminated Spirit) and Wealth position (activated by water) is in the east (as *Lo Shu* 3 = *Ho Tu* 8).

S

3 8 1	8 4 6	1 6 8
2 4 6	7 9 2	9 2 4
7 9 5	3 5 1	5 7 3

E

2 7 9	4 9 2	6 2 4
3 5 5	3 5 7	5 7 9
8 6 4	8 1 6	1 3 8

W

7 3 5	9 5 7	5 1 3
6 8 1	8 1 3	4 6 8
2 4 9	4 6 2	9 2 7

N

The *Mountain Star* (in the *Sitting Palace* i.e. back wall) represents the retaining *Yin Qi* of a building, denoting health and family harmony; the *Water Star* (in the *Facing Palace*) represents the *Yang Qi* entering a building, and prosperity. These, monthly and daily Stars can also be centred and flown for detailed readings of Star nature, timeliness, and element combinations in each trigram sector.

STAR	1	2	3	4	5	6	7	8	9
Colour	White	Black	Jade	Green	Yellow	White	Red	White	Purple
Star	Tan Lang	Ju Men	Lu Cun	Wen Qu	Lian Zhen	Wu Qu	Po Jun	Zhou Fu	Yu Bi
Translation	Greedy Wolf	Officer at the Gate	Preserver of Rank	Literary Pursuits	Purity in Truth	Military Pursuits	Destroyer of Armies	Left Supporter	Right Supporter
Yin/Yang	○	○		○	●	○		●	●
Element	Wood	Earth	Earth	Water	Fire	Metal	Metal	Wood	Wood
Gua	Zhen	Gen	Kun	Kan	Li	Qian	Dui	Xun	Xun
Fortune	Ausp.	Inausp.	Varies	Ausp	Power	Ausp	Varies	Ausp	Power
Yun	1864	1884	1904	1924	1944	1964	1984	2004	2024
Portent	Sheng Qi	Tian Yi	Huo Hai	Liu Sha	Wu Gui	Yen Nian	Jue Ming	Fu Wei	Fu Wei
Translation	Fertile Qi	Heaven's Will	Mishap	Six Curses	Five Ghosts	Long Life	Severed Fate	Throne	Throne
Land -Form									

APPENDIX VIII – 8 HOUSE PORTENTS

The Eight Portents, listed below, are derived from the trigram in which the house sits (i.e. the back of the house) to read health, and from the facing trigram to read wealth. Use the chart (right) to identify these two *Lo Shu* numbers, their trigrams, and the grid of Portent directions for each trigram. The Portents define room use, Element cures (controlling or draining to the negative Portent element) and enhancements (nourishing or same element to positive Portents).

To construct a *Ming Gua* (personal Natal Trigram) chart: i) Add 1 to the year of birth if born after Winter Solstice. ii) For males, divide the last two digits of the birth year by 9 and note the remainder (if the remainder is 0 read it as 9), then subtract it from 10 (or from 9 if born after 2000) to find the *Ming Gua*. iii) For females add 5 to the last two digits of the birth year (or 6 if born after 2000), divide by 9 and the remainder is the *Ming Gua*. iv) If the *Ming Gua* is 5 it becomes 2 for males, 8 for females. The *Later Heaven Ba Gua* Trigram relating to this number via the *Lo Shu* is the *Natal Trigram*, and defines which of the eight grids to choose from.

1. *SHENG QI* is the best portent, energizing, bringing good fortune and prosperity to business and personal life; being in the right place at the right time. A good area and orientation for the front door, bedroom, living room, study, or creative work space.

2. *TIAN YI* brings spiritual and physical healing, financial regeneration, and cures bad luck and evil influence. Good for a therapy room or sick person's bedroom, and the best direction for the *Fire Mouth*, or door of the kitchen stove to face.

3. *HUO HAI* is the weakest of the unlucky portents, bringing minor accidents, money loss, legal disputes, contagious diseases, worry and irritability. Best used for kitchen, bathroom or storage.

4. *LIU SHA* brings accidents, illness, financial & legal

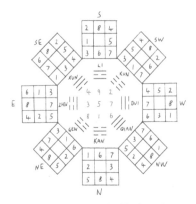

problems, lost *Qi* and the death of family members or employees. Best for kitchen, toilet, or storage.

5. *WU GUI* is associated with hauntings, burglary, fires, quarrels, betrayal, loss of employees, legal and financial loss, and injury to the youngest child - best used for kitchen or toilet, though positively aspected good for a shrine or work with spirit guides.

6. *YEN NIAN* represents longevity & harmonious family relations. Activating this area enables relationships, cures quarrels and infertility, and ensures rich descendants - a good area for family, dining and bedrooms.

7. *JUE MING* is the worst portent, and can bring redundancy, bankruptcy, divorce, persistent poor health and death, "all descendants die and the family name is lost", if activated by underground, form or astrological *Sha*. Use for toilet or storage.

8. *FU WEI* represents the throne, one's basic self and personal path, clear thinking, a harmonious and favourable life, and strong protection against bad luck. A good area if well protected for the front door or main bedroom, study, and desk orientation.

APPENDIX IX – YI JING

1. *Qian*. The Creative. Activity and perseverance in what is right brings sublime success.

2. *Kun*. The Receptive. Following guidance and subtle action brings good fortune.

3. *Tun*. Sprouting. Fragility at the beginning, furthering through perseverance.

4. *Meng*. Youthful Folly. Success, though enthusiasm should be tempered with discipline.

5. *Xu*. Waiting. Good outcome is possible with politeness and circumspection.

6. *Song*. Dispute. Confidence obstructs, compromise and wise advice bring good fortune.

7. *Shi*. The Multitude. Guidance by responsible leadership has good fortune.

8. *Bi*. Union. Timely cooperation from the start is fortunate. Those who are uncertain gradually join.

9. *Xiao Chu*. A Small Offering. Restraint and attention to necessary details fulfil plans.

10. *Lu*. Walking. Good conduct brings success and no harm, though treading on the tiger's tail.

11. *Tai*. Great. Peaceful prosperity, Heaven and Earth unite in harmony. An end to all feuds.

12. *Pi*. To Close. Stop, inferior people are in ascent, change the obstruction or yourself.

13. *Tong Ren*. Union of Men. Group effort and participation in projects brings profit.

14. *Da You*. Great Possessions. Great wealth, honour the spiritual realms and offer charity.

15. *Qian*. Modesty. Reverence and offerings can harmonise events.

16. *Yu*. Pleasure. Easy movement with forethought and prearrangement. Install helpers.

17. *Sui*. Following. Following form and experience is advantageous. To rule, first learn to serve.

18. *Gu*. Poison. A Great offering, preparation and reflection are required to correct deficiencies.

19. *Lin*. Approach. Advancing brings great success, arrival must be within eight months.

20. *Guan*. Observation. Sincerity, dignity and spiritual cleansing bring rewards.

21. *Shi He*. Punishment. Biting and chewing through problems is difficult but rewarding.

22. *Bi*. Decoration. Small successes and minor goals achieved with outward refinement.

23. *Bo*. Stripping. Vulnerability, examine the true skeleton, it is best to stay still at home.

24. *Fu*. Return. Movement is advantageous, return to the Dao without urgency.

25. *Wu Wang*. Innocence. Movement with ignorance brings misfortune, correctness good.

26. *Da Chu*. Great Restraint. Offer large charitable gifts and feast in good company.

27. *Yi*. Nourishment. Attend to quality and quantity of nourishment for yourself and others.

28. *Da Guo*. Extraordinary. Measures greatly beyond the ordinary are called for.

29. *Kan*. Abyss. Dangerous waters, heart-centred action has honour.

30. *Li*. Brightness. Fiery intelligence and correct action profits, nurture male & female equally.

31. *Xian*. Influence. Coming together brings joyful success, listen to mind, heart and body.

32. *Heng*. Constancy. Endurance and perseverance bring regularity and stability.

33. *Dun*. Hiding. Conceal assets from ascendant dark forces, and virtuous actions with modesty.

34. *Da Zhuang*. Great Strength. Power is only useful with intelligence and timeliness.

35. *Jin*. Advance. Flourishing prosperity, tempered with virtue and caution as all is transient.

36. *Ming Yi*. Brightness Obscured. In adversity, hide your light to take advantage of problems.

37. *Jia Ren*. Family. With family responsibilities and virtue in order, all is well.

38. *Kui*. Strange. Unsual circumstances, but no misfortune in small matters. Discord will not benefit.

39. *Jian*. Difficulty. Pause and seek wise counsel, let events take their course.

40. *Jie*. Loosen. Danger abating, establish a good location and let goals arive.

41. *Sun*. Decrease. Even with slender means, sincerity and inner offering is substantial.

42. *Yi*. Increase. Every action will bring earthly prosperity and spiritual flowering.

43. *Quai*. Decision. Define goals, strategy and a place to go to establish a stong position.

44. *Gou*. Coupling. Meeting in sexual congress, female too powerful to marry.

45. *Cui*. Gathering together. Commune with others, spiritual powers, and self through sacrifice.

46. *Sheng*. Ascend. Communication with Heaven, sacrifice, put one's house in order.

47. *Kun*. Distress. Confinement, tiredness and lost trust demand reverence and wise counsel.

48. *Jing*. The well. Nature is constant, human structures require the responsibility of mutual care.

49. *Ge*. Change. Shedding a skin, personal internal transformation, with confidence.

50. *Ding*. Cauldron. Make works of art as human and spiritual gifts, alchemical transformation.

51. *Zhen*. Arousing. Waves of thunder bring fright and laughter, sacrifice and ritual maintain calm.

52. *Gen*. Stillness. Meditation and transcendant consciousness, power comes from being still.

53. *Jian*. Development. Move gradually when performing actions of bonding.

54. *Gui Mei*. Marrying maiden. Imposition of service, undertakings bring misfortune.

55. *Feng*. Abundance. Paranormal spiritual vision brings rewards of future prosperity.

56. *Lu*. Traveller. Pay respects to the spirits for a safe journey and good fortune. Do not be overbearing.

57. *Xun*. Gentle. Wise counsel, a small offering, and discipline bring gradual rewards.

58. *Dui*. Joyful. Take pleasure and profit in the moment, rejoice in giving and receiving

59. *Huan*. Disperse. Expand into new territory for gain, protection and insight. Dissolve egotism.

60. *Jie*. Regulations. Ensure rules are not too restrictive, but are in accord with the Dao.

61. *Zhong Fu*. Inner Sincerity. Success in major actions, maintain inner centredness.

62. *Xiao Guo*. Small and Extraordinary. If small details are supported, great good fortune.

63. *Ji Ji*. Already Completed. Small actions bring good fortune if timely, disorder if late.

64. *Wei Ji*. Not Yet Completed. No profit until the end, yet no event is ever truly complete.

Sixth Yao, uppermost stroke: Gods, Ancestors
Fifth Yao, middle of top trigram: Emperor
Fourth Yao, fourth stroke: Mandarin, Noble

Third Yao, top of lower trigram: Magistrate
Second Yao, second stroke: Official
First Yao, lowest line: Layman

APPENDIX X – ANIMAL SYMBOLISM

TORTOISE: Represents deep spiritual wisdom, longevity and strength. Most auspicious placed in the north of home.

DRAGON: Symbolises benevolent power, good fortune, the essence of strength, goodness & blessings; best in east.

PHOENIX: Sun and purification, virtue, peace and prosperity; best in the south. A Phoenix and Dragon together symbolise the Empress and Emperor, and are especially auspicious for marriage, as are a pair of fish or mandarin **DUCKS**.

TIGER: Majesty, ferocity, courage. Guards house from evil. Best in the west, facing away from house, lest it eat inhabitants.

FISH: Brings abundance, fertility, wealth and success; best in the north, near front door, or in the living room.

ELEPHANT: Brings strength, sagacity, prosperity and power, and is best in the east.

LION: Majesty and courage. Guards house from evil when placed outside main gate or door in pairs. On the right side (looking out) it is female and may have a foot on a baby lion, for family protection. On the left it is male and may have a foot on a sphere, symbolising the sun and spiritual protection. Best in the south.

UNICORN: brings happiness, good fortune, wisdom, goodness and longevity, and is exalted in the west.

SNAKE: Symbolises wisdom, the deep secrets of life, and is auspicious in the north and centre.

STORK: Signifies longevity, fertility and family harmony and is best in the south-east, south and south-west.

HORSE Represents speed, strength, high status and good repute and is best in the south.

FROG / TOAD: Calls down moon, rain and money. Best in the SW, W, NW or unobtrusively inside facing front door.

APPENDIX XI – PRONOUNCING PINYIN

Consonants.

Like English, except for:

x like the *s* in *see* + the *sh* in *she*. Smile when you say it!

z like *ds* in *words*.

r like *r* in *raw*, with your tongue curled back.

c like *ts* in *eats*.

q like *ch* in *cheat*.

j like the *dj* in *jam*, with minimal exhalation.

ng like the *ng* in *song*.

zh like *dg* in *sludge*.

sh like the *sh* in *wash*, with tongue curled back.

Single Vowels

a like the *a* in *far*.

o is like *or*.

e like the *e* in *send* or *very*. Except when a single vowel follows a consonant, then more like *ir* in *bird*.

i as in *sit*. Except when preceded by *c*, *s* or *z*, then like a mosquito ... *ziiiii*.

u like the *oo* in *loop*.

Vowel Combinations

an Like a soft *an* in *ban*.

ang *a* + *ng*.

ao is like *ow* in *cow*.

ei is like *ay* in *bay*.

en like the *en* in *taken*. .

eng is like *ung* in *sung*.

er is like *ur* in *purse*.

ia is like *ya*.

iang *y* + *ang*

ie is like a tight *yeh*.

iu is like the *ou* in *you*.

ian like *yen*.

iao like *eow* in *meow*.

in like the *in* in *gin*.

ing like the *ing* in *sing*.

iong is like *eyong*.

ong as in *kong*.

ou is like *ow* in *low*.

ua is like *ua* in *guava*.

uan *u* + *an*.

uang is like *oo* + *ang*.

ui is like *way*.

un is like *wou* in *would* + *n*.

uo is like *war*.

uai is like *why*.

ue is like *oo-eh*

NB. This is not the complete Pinyin system. It is a guide to aid pronunciation of the Chinese terms in this book.